SCHOLASTIC
News
Nonfiction Readers

A Home on the Prairie

By David C. Lion

Children's Press®
A Division of Scholastic Inc.
New York Toronto London Auckland Sydney
Mexico City New Delhi Hong Kong
Danbury, Connecticut

These content vocabulary word builders are for grades 1–2.

Subject Consultant: Susan Woodward, Professor of Geography, Radford University, Radford, Virginia

Reading Consultant: Cecilia Minden-Cupp, PhD, Former Director of the Language and Literacy Program, Harvard Graduate School of Education, Cambridge, Massachusetts

Photographs © 2007: Dembinsky Photo Assoc.: 23 bottom right (Bill Leaman), 5 top left, 11, 23 top right (Gary Meszaros), 1, 5 bottom left, 8 (G. Alan Nelson), 21 bottom (Rod Planck), cover background (Richard Hamilton Smith); Minden Pictures/Jim Brandenburg: cover left inset, 5 top right, 7, 14; Nature Picture Library Ltd./Jeff Foott: 19; Peter Arnold Inc./Tom Vezo: cover right inset, 2, 4 bottom left, 17; Photo Researchers, NY: 4 top right, 12 (Steve Cooper), 23 bottom left, 23 top left (Jeffrey Lepore), 15 (Craig K. Lorenz), 20 bottom (Gary Meszaros), 20 top (Nature's Images), cover center inset, 4 bottom right, 13 (Art Wolfe), 21 top (Jim Zipp); Tom Bean: back cover, 5 bottom right, 9.

Book Design: Simonsays Design!
Book Production: The Design Lab

Library of Congress Cataloging-in-Publication Data

Lion, David C., 1948–
   A home on the prairie / by David C. Lion.
      p. cm. — (Scholastic news nonfiction readers)
   Includes index.
   ISBN-10: 0-516-25346-8
   ISBN-13: 978-0-516-25346-6
   1. Prairie ecology—Juvenile literature. I. Title. II. Series.
QH541.5.P7L56 2006
577.4'4—dc22   2006002308

2 3 4 5 6 7 8 9 10 R 16 15 14 13 12 11 10 09 08

CONTENTS

WORD HUNT

Look for these words as you read. They will be in **bold**.

American bison
(uh-**mer**-uh-kuhn **bye**-suhn)

colonies
(**kol**-uh-neez)

grazers
(**grayz**-urz)

bluestem
(**blu**-stehm)

burrows
(**bur**-ohz)

habitat
(**hab**-uh-tat)

prairie
(**prer**-ee)

5

What Is This Place?

Just imagine you're surrounded by tall grass. When you look up, you see nothing but sky.

You hear a rattlesnake shake its tail. You watch a prairie dog dive into a hole.

Where are we?

A rattlesnake shakes its tail to warn its enemies.

We're on a North American **prairie**!

A prairie is a type of **habitat**. A habitat is where a plant or animal usually lives.

A prairie is a large, open grassland with almost no trees.

habitat

Prairies have very few trees.

Many different kinds of grasses grow on the prairie. There are tallgrass, mixed-grass, and short-grass prairies.

Bluestem and Indian grass are the tallest grasses on the prairie.

Bluestem can grow eight feet tall! That's much taller than most adults.

American bison roam the prairies. Another name for bison is buffalo.

Bison and deer are prairie **grazers**, which means they feed on prairie grasses.

American bison

Deer graze on grass, leaves, bark, and acorns.

Many prairie animals live in underground holes called **burrows**. Badgers, black-footed ferrets, prairie dogs, and burrowing owls all spend time in these holes.

burrow

Most owls live in trees. But burrowing owls live in underground holes!

Prairie dog burrows connect to form groups, or **colonies**. These colonies are almost like underground towns.

Prairie dogs got their name from the loud barking noise they make.

The prairie is an exciting place to explore! Peek among the tall grasses. You'll meet this black-footed ferret and other truly amazing animals that live in this habitat!

A DAY IN THE LIFE OF A RATTLESNAKE

How does a rattlesnake spend most of its time? A rattlesnake hides in burrows or under rocks or plants.

What does a rattlesnake eat? A rattlesnake eats mice, ground squirrels, and younger prairie dogs and rabbits.

What are a rattlesnake's enemies?

Humans, hawks, and eagles are a rattlesnake's enemies.

Does a rattlesnake have a special survival trick?
A rattlesnake rattles its tail as a warning to stay away.

YOUR NEW WORDS

American bison (uh-**mer**-uh-kuhn **bye**-suhn) prairie animals with large heads and high, humped shoulders

bluestem (**blu**-stehm) one of the tallest types of prairie grass

burrows (**bur**-ohz) holes or tunnels in the ground that are made by a small animal

colonies (**kol**-uh-neez) groups of animals that live in one place

grazers (**grayz**-urz) animals that feed on growing grasses

habitat (**hab**-uh-tat) the place where a plant or animal usually lives

prairie (**prer**-ee) a large, open grassland with very few trees

OTHER ANIMALS THAT LIVE ON THE PRAIRIE

bobcats

elks

foxes

meadowlarks

INDEX

FIND OUT MORE

Book:

Zuchora-Walske, Christine. *Peeking Prairie Dogs.* Minneapolis: Lerner, 1999.

Website:

Environmental Education for Kids: What Is a Prairie?
http://www.dnr.state.wi.us/org/caer/ce/eek/nature/habitat/whatprai.htm

MEET THE AUTHOR:

David Lion is a retired school teacher and author of children's books. He lives with his wife, Kathy, and their cat, Jeep, in Glens Falls, New York. When not writing, David can be found on his bass boat, on the golf course, or reading to his granddaughter.